Heaven Sent
Gifts from Above

Inspirational Poems and Short
Stories from a Man of God

Jim McClelland

WESTBOW
PRESS
A DIVISION OF THOMAS NELSON

WestBow Press books may be ordered through booksellers or by contacting:

WestBow Press
A Division of Thomas Nelson
1663 Liberty Drive
Bloomington, IN 47403
www.westbowpress.com
1-(866) 928-1240

ISBN: 978-1-4497-8820-9 (sc)
ISBN: 978-1-4497-8821-6 (e)

Library of Congress Control Number: 2013904523

Printed in the United States of America

WestBow Press rev. date: 3/11/2013

The joy of writing is not given only to the elite, the intellect, or the gifted. The joy of writing begins within the heart. And the joy of writing is completed as the desire to give birth to memories from the personal experience is inked.

-Jim McClelland

TABLE OF CONTENTS

ACKNOWLEDGMENTS

This, my first attempt to pen words upon paper, is an experience I will always cherish. The first encounter with gathering together words from my random thoughts came early one morning in the fall of 2004. I was awakened with just two words, Consider Life, and the more I tried to find sleep again, the more the words called out to me.

I give sincere thanks to my wife, Janice, for her patience with me during late night hours when I would ask her to read the most recent gathering of words.

Without her help, I could not have finished this humble beginning of the joy of writing.

Jim McClelland
February 2005

Jimmy Dale McClelland and Janice Ann Poe at their 8th grade Sadie Hawkin's Day "Wedding"

PROLOGUE
Assurance

When I slow down and reflect on the "important", I find myself remembering the past and its foundation built upon my faith in God.

When I am alone and consider "next steps", I am reminded of God's faithfulness during times of uncertainty and sincere questions.

When I think of how God has covered me with His favor and gifted me by His grace, I am moved within my body...my throat seems to close tightly around unspoken words.

When the warm, salty tears of emotion flow slowly down my face, I am comforted by the scripture, "Cast your cares upon Him, for He cares for you".

When I try to understand the totality of God, I again am comforted with His scripture, "Trust the Lord with all your heart and lean not upon your own understanding, in all your ways acknowledge Him, and He will make your paths straight".

When I need strength for the future I am amazed that the Creator reminds me of the most important and comforting "absolute", God is my Father, He loves me, and He is moving within my life…for my best!

When I wonder what to do next…I must remind myself to do three things; don't worry, trust in God's Word, and smile!

Consider Life

Consider life; its purpose, its quest
Is it future, is it now, or is it simply a guess
Life before, life present, or our life's future request
Dare we ever consider what might be life's very best

Are we alone, together, or searching for home
Can we find pleasure in silence, the quiet unknown
Are we searching for meaning thru outward content
Holding tightly to the memory of times already spent

Have you found the point of your personal success
Pressing forward, or living with fear and regress
Are your dreams still alive and continually inspired
Or choose to live a life where success is often denied

I choose to seek life's bounty filled with its very best
Friends who are faithful during life's challenging tests
Families committed to love in failure, and even success
Remember god offers to all, an unearned, eternal rest

Consider life; it's purpose, its quest
It is the future, the now, and it is not a simple guess
I have determined to seek God's very best
God offers Peace, Comfort, and His loving Caress

Scriptures For Life...

"**D**on't fret or worry. Instead of worrying, pray. Let petitions and praises shape your worries into prayers, letting God know your concerns. Before you know it, a sense of God's wholeness, everything coming together for good, will come and settle you down. It's wonderful what happens when Christ displaces worry at the center of your life." Philippians 4:6, 7 (MSG)

These scriptures were our foundation when Janice, Matt, Amie, and I cut the family "umbilical cord", left Jonesboro, Arkansas, and moved to Cape Girardeau, Missouri. How does a husband, a father, and a man who changes his career path respond to "don't worry"? I can only describe it as the beginning of the most peaceful assurance which could ever be coveted. When worry knocks, I just don't answer the door!

"Trust God from the bottom of your heart; don't try to figure out everything on your own. Listen for God's voice in everything you do, everywhere you go; he's the one who will keep you on track." Proverbs 3:4, 5 (MSG)

Moving from Jonesboro, Arkansas to Cape Girardeau, Missouri was a major event for a young husband and father, but moving to Hartford, Connecticut at the mature age of 50 is another thing! Leaving all, going into a "foreign land" was almost more than Janice could handle. But God is always faithful. During our stay in New England we were again gifted with a family of friends who became as dear as our birth family.

"I know what I'm doing. I have it all planned out; plans to take care of you, not abandon you, plans to give you the future you hope for." Jeremiah 29:11 (MSG)

I will not go into great detail, but this move from Hartford, Connecticut to Rochester, New York had to be God's plan; we had little if any input with this one. But God remains faithful. Here in New York we have the flexibility to not only be "who we truly are", but the freedom to become "whom God has graciously planned"!

Maybe, just maybe, I will soon be writing a new scripture which will introduce the next journey for Janice and Jim McClelland. DON'T WORRY…when it happens you will be one of the firsts to know!

Momma's Kitchen

A fresh aroma enters my room each morn
The room from which it comes is not overly adorned
Its contents are many and some are even antiques
Its creations would enhance many elegant boutiques

The master of this room is meticulous and caring
The cookies on the counter are there for the sharing
Within the walls of this great room echo words of wisdom
Within this room humility is seen more often than seldom

When asked to retrieve important tools, aids or objects
I'm directed to a place, holding answers for various subjects
What... Why... or where in the world is that thing-of-a-jig
It's in the drawer, second from the top, left side of the frig

As the years have passed and I look back on my life
I am reminded of a place where peace existed, absent of strife
It is always warm there, even in January
It's the kitchen; my mamma's sanctuary

I learned to give and receive there in a wonderful way
May I have a cookie, of course, but go outside to play
Yes, mom, I will and if I've forgotten to say
Thank you for being so kind, you deserve a beautiful bouquet

The Clog

I recently visited one of those stores which sell odds 'n ins no longer wanted by the original owner. The adventure was planned by my wife and one of her friends. Not to be taken in by this useless waste of time, I decided to find an item which would peak my interest and force me to research its origin or unique purpose.

After searching for what seemed to be eternity I spotted the item, hidden almost out of sight from a normal shopper... "treasure-hunter". **A clog**; not a pair, but a single wooden shoe. Why would this item catch my eye, I'm not sure! I had no idea of its unique purpose or origin, therefore my plan was accomplished.

"That will be fifty-two cents", the customer service person said with a loud and coarse voice. It seemed as if everyone within twenty feet of me turned to see what I had purchased for fifty-two cents. I guess to spend such a large sum of money in a place like this was unheard of.

The clog, worn by poor workers during the Industrial Revolution in France, England, Belgium, Luxembourg and the Netherlands; the clog, worn by ladies of fashion while walking through muddy city streets; **the clog**, even worn by Queen Mary II; the clog, worn by Catherine Morland in Jane Austen's "Northanger Abbey"; **the clog**, worn by Mrs. Perrybingle in "The Cricket on the Hearth"; **the clog**, discovered in the tombs of ancient Egyptians; **the clog**, worn by both men and women in the hot baths in Rome; **the clog**, worn by Mid-Victorian dancers; **the clog**, worn by Charlie Chaplain as he danced with J.W. Jackson's Eight Lancashire Lads; **the clog**, most often thought of only as Dutch footwear is displayed in my office to remind me of a most important fact.

Our humble beginnings can and should be an opportunity to become not only worthwhile but desirable, sought after, and needed by many.

Listening

A mother awakens, hears her baby crying, leaves the comfort of sleep, and moves quickly to quiet the fear or anxiety of her child. Is it a gift, an inner awareness, or the learned art of listening...maybe each one of the three is used within different occasions. As a child, have you ever cried out to your mother and her response was simply, "go to sleep". Later, "mother I need a drink of water", was rewarded with a cool drink, a lullaby, and momma staying close until you had fallen fast asleep.

How did she know I was afraid, seeing the moon's glow creating shadows on the bedroom wall and offered a reassuring hug or tender words to obliterate my fear? Did God gift mother with a special "knowing"? Did mother see the same shadows on her wall and feel some of the same inner discomfort or had mother learned from my older sister that nervous-sounding words needed special attention? Don't know the answers to all of the questions, but one thing is certain... momma almost every time heard more than what I was saying or thinking. Momma seemed to hear what I was feeling, wanting, and what was the true meaning of my message.

Oh how I need to listen more!

A father watches his son or daughter take a bottom of the 9th inning called third strike which was the last out of the inning. A loss is recorded in the record book for his child's team. As the child retreats to the dugout several body gestures tell a story; the father listens intently with his eyes. The body language communicated by the child gives dad the insight needed to communicate during the trip home, a nice place to enjoy dinner, or off to another event.

How did dad know I was afraid, seeing the expressions on the faces of my teammates, and wondering if my friends hated me for my failure to win the game? "Great game..., the two run double you hit in the third inning was sweet", caused me to remember my double was the hit which put us ahead by one run! Even though we didn't win every time we took the field, Dad always spoke words of encouragement when I needed them the most.

Oh how I need to listen more!

Listening is more than just hearing words spoken by others. Body language, if you listen with your eyes, will speak louder and more accurately than the spoken word. Often we hear the words, but fail to hear the message. Others' hopes, dreams, wants, and needs are distorted by cold hard facts.

We are taught to tell the truth, the whole truth, and nothing but the truth. We are also taught to be courteous and caring; sometimes TRUTH hurts and we compromise TRUTH by using words which will hide our true feelings and emotions. Try this! During the upcoming days, decide to listen with your heart and eyes, as well as your ears! Listen for TRUTHS concealed just below the surface of "conversation".

The Face of a Child

Today I looked into the face of a child
So fragile, so innocent; I couldn't help but smile
The beginning of life without even one care
It is a sight that all of us should be willing to share.

If you are blessed with a daughter or son
You know they're a gift of which the value is unknown
For we cherish their life with an unfailing love
For we know the gift was given from heaven above.

And the best of life is yet to come
For our child will be blessed with one of their own
To hold close, hold tight, without even one care
It's their gift from heaven, with us to share.

So tonight before you fall fast asleep
Thank the Giver for the gifts He's asked you to keep
Safe and warm always wrapped in the arms of love
For we know the gifts were given from heaven above.

The Greatest Gift... Thank You God!

Happy Birthday

I know you are getting a card from your mother with an article which she read and thought of you while she was reading. Regretfully, I don't take the time to read as much as I should.

"I like to create the articles"
So imagine a famous writer wrote this just for YOU!

Seldom is there born into this world a person who exemplifies the grace and beauty of God's creation,

Seldom is there born into this world a person who mirrors the love and caring nature of God,

Seldom is there born into this world a person who offers joy, comfort, and peace which comes from God,

Seldom is there born into this world a person who embraces life and living as God designed,

Seldom is there born into this world a person who brings such pleasure and delight to her parents,

Seldom is there born into this world a person who is so SPECIAL, but it happened thirty-two years ago!

With All My Love! Dad

A Much Needed Walk

Most evenings I take a much-needed walk
I choose to be quiet and seldom ever talk
It's a time that I need to be alone and consider
What's important; see the future a little clearer

I have friends I walk with each and every day
My old sweatshirt, baggy pants; I'm on my way
Comfort is my goal as I tie those old shoes
Style is not important as I walk away my blues

At first it's not fun walking the same old route
My mood changes; the children's smiles are so cute
It's the children and my friends who stop to wave
It's their love, acceptance; not the walk I crave

The exercise is needed to sustain my good health
But others' love I understand is a great wealth
My body will change and my strength will decline
But the love from my friends will forever be mine.

I turn the last corner knowing soon I'll be home
I recall the place of my youth I used to call home
It was safe, filled with love, and I was at peace
At that moment I begin to feel a sense of release.
Now I'm someone whom others depend upon for love
I must welcome them with a smile; even a hug

The secret of receiving is found in the art of giving
Life filled with love for others is a life worth living

Loose sweatshirts, baggy pants; those old shoes
Are friends that help me as I search for the clues
To live a life that brings purpose and pleasure
Old friends are like wealth; our purest treasure.

Life

The evening sunset silently commands shadows from the cottonwood to disappear and welcomes a darkening haze over the landscape. Robins sprint to capture the unsuspecting slow-moving earthworm just beneath the fresh mown lawn's canopy. Time relaxes, neighborhood sounds wane, and calm sneaks in just before evening.

Today's stress, tomorrow's anxiety, and future's questions are mute. The wicker rocker offers its comfortable support for the weary body. Shoe laces are loosened and a sweat soaked cap is removed. A deep breath is expelled; the work day is almost over.

To give all of one's self while reaching for selfless achievement is rewarded with personal awareness of a job well done. How can any human-being not strive for their best, yearn forward for more challenges, and laugh inwardly when accomplishments are recognized. Today's forward movements are ending; giving way for tomorrow's next steps.

When life seems common, lack-luster, or cumbersome one needs to look eagerly for the morning's horizon and embrace its opportunities. An authentic heartfelt greeting to the unknown passerby, a smile created by eye-to-eye contact with someone serving you coffee, and of course that look of self-worth as the reflection from the mirror becomes appreciated.

Life is a collection of events which trigger the need to choose; to be the best we can be, or less than the reason of our birth. Life is a gift to be cherished but also given away for the benefit of others. Life is filled with responsibilities to love, forgive, and be forgiven.

LIFE is:

Living In Full Expectation!

Expecting to Love and to be Loved!

Forgive freely and willingly!

And Forgiveness accepted when offered!

My Ole Rocking Chair...

It was an old rocking chair, just like the one we relax in after a delicious meal at Cracker Barrel. The morning spring showers, the hot summer sun, the cool autumn frost, and the cold winter snow had left their own unique fingerprints on this old chair. One rocker had become loose and with each movement forward the squeak from wood rubbing against wood broke the silence that day.

My mind drifted in and out of what some would call a trance while others might describe it as a lazy day-dream. This ole rocking chair had become more to me than a place to relax; it was my "SANCTUARY". When there were questions about life's difficulties and future challenges, this is where I came.

I would search through memories, lessons learned from both good and less than good. I would revisit counsel given from past and present mentors, but most of the time I would simply talk to God. I learned quickly that my vocabulary did not have to be expansive or eloquent, just honest words spoken from a needy person into the ear of the Creator.

This ole rocking chair had felt the weight of a father who wondered if his children were OK when the clock in the kitchen moved its hands passed the agreed upon time for their homecoming. This ole rocking chair had absorbed many salty tears which dropped from eyes of thanksgiving when life seemed to be more than I could have ever dreamed. But most of the time this ole rocking chair supported a tired and weak man who often thought he held the weight of the whole world, all alone.

Late one afternoon I was "day-dreaming" as I squeaked back and forth. Just over my left shoulder a wonderful little boy hesitated as he stepped toward me. My son was a gentle and polite young man seldom requiring special attention. He was not shy, but respectfully quiet. I knew he would be entering a very competitive life very soon, so I inwardly hoped he would become a little more self- confident.

I wanted him to boldly move toward me, get my attention, ask the question he wanted to ask, defend his question, and convince me that his request was worthwhile. For a few seconds; it seemed to me an hour or more, he stood there completely motionless.

As he began to retreat from my presence, I said, "Hey Bud, what do you need", felling guilty for ignoring him. The he said these words which, still to this day even as I write, brings tears to my eyes, "Nothing Dad, it's not really important, I don't want to bother you". With arms outstretched I invited him to sit in my lap. I wanted him to experience the confidence and assurance of "SANCTUARY" which I enjoyed each time I sat there in that ole rocking chair.

His request was easily fulfilled; it was within my power to grant, it was no bother, and it took little effort to supply his need! We laughed and talked for a time and very soon he was off my lap hurrying inside to tell his mother of his success; JUST TALKING TO DAD. Silently I wished he could realize that a father wanted his children to trust enough, not to be afraid, and take their needs and wants and sit in his lap and simply ASK.

I have never heard the audible voice of God; but that day I knew for sure He was speaking directly to me. In the inner most part of my heart I heard God say, "Why don't you trust Me enough and never fear coming to Me with ALL of your needs and wants".

I have learned parents can learn a lot from their children..., and from that very day until now I confidently walk up to God, figuratively, and ask knowing He will not withhold any good thing from me.

My son is a man now and commands not only respect, but also admiration from those who cross his path. Through the humble example of a father's outstretched arms, he has found his own "SANCTUARY" in the trust and confidence which only comes from God. You just might want to find a place of your own, and call it your "SANCTUARY"! Bring the weight of your world and roll the cares of your world over on the Father; He is never too busy to listen.

Congratulations

You were wrapped in a warm blanket, your face was a little flushed, and the nurse held you carefully as she brought you close to the window of the nursery room. It was the first time in my life I truly knew the "love of God". Our first born, Matthew Blake, had just entered this world. And I was the proud father!

You are covered with the favor of God, your future is without limits, and your mother and I are proud of your commitment to God's desire for the rest of your life. And I am the proud father!

Humble arrogance, the confidence to be "who you are", is keeping you flexible and also secure. Your willingness to embrace any/all challenges, as well as your ability to manage change allows uninhibited growth in all areas of your life. And I continue to be the proud father!

Congratulations on your continued success!

The Sanctuary

The sun had begun its decent behind a horizon enclosed in gold-plated amber clouds. Layers of warm soft clothing imprisoned my body's temperature as I departed our home to visit nature's "sanctuary" only A Short Walk beyond our backyard. A snow shower fashioned a backdrop which hindered the typical view of the trees and underbrush. One surrounded by the woods the falling snow was dispersed by the leafless limbs of the trees; my focus was clear and my steps were silent.

A narrow path meandered through dissimilar landscapes; swamp-like areas with shallow pools of water invited a multitude of animals, higher ridges filled with evergreens offered defense from unforgiving winter winds, and tall Oaks yielded nourishing food for the deer and squirrels. Slowly and quietly I moved to a location where all crossroads of the woods convened.

Within the shallow water a family of raccoons searched for their evening meal. Squirrels seemed to fly from limb to limb of the Oaks celebrating their cash-crop of acorns. Without warning, twigs began to break beneath measured but deliberate steps from the evergreens. For a moment the breaking of the twigs was sound-proofed by the riotous beating of my heart. I froze; not from the outdoor air temperature but from immense personal anticipation. It's the buck; the one which formed those large circular scrapes in the ground which mark his territory.

The trail has become his corridor from the adjacent corn field where he fees to the evergreens used as an ideal bedding area. Within heart-beats the six point buck crossed directly in front of me; abut thirty yards away. As quickly as he appeared, he vanished; the darkness of the evening had overtaken my vision. If only for a second or two, the experience of witnessing the movement of "the buck" was worthwhile.

There will be another day, another evening, another time for our paths to cross. He was aware of my presence; for I am only a visitor within his "sanctuary".

Just a Moment

Just a moment, a minute, a measure of time
A smile, a wink, a friendly gesture of mine
A glance, a look, not knowing just why
Thank you, you're welcome, a courteous reply

I wonder how often I've passed you by
Without saying a word, I know I should try
To encourage each person whomever I meet
As I hurry to work or just crossing the street

Just a moment, a minute, a measure of time
Time is so valuable and you know it's really mine
To enjoy the special things I like to do
Sometimes I'm just too busy to share time with you

Don't be sad, mad, or upset with me
I'm so busy with important stuff, you see
Maybe tomorrow, next week, or in a month or two
We will spend time together, just me and you

Just a moment, a minute, a measure of time
Let's have coffee, a roll... how about tomorrow at nine
Can't make it... Oh you've got something important to do
But... we are such good friends... me and you
That's OK, maybe next week or in a month or two
I really miss the time I used to share with you

Don't forget me; I don't want to lose a good friend
Friends are special; to lose one would be such a sin

Just a moment, a minute, time is a gift from heaven above
To share unhindered with those whom we love

Time Is Priceless... Share It With Others

A Safe Place

I am sure I learned this from my father; you know the way we look into a mirror while we have our back to another mirror to see the back of our head. Almost every time my dad would finish giving someone a haircut, he would give them a mirror and turn the barber chair around so they could see the back of their head. "How 'bout that", he would inquire.

How often have you set the timer on the oven for 40 minutes; that's about the average time one of those Duncan Hines cake mix boxes tells us to bake a cake, and then open the oven door 10 minutes early just to look inside to see if the cake is baking? Have you ever said, "Oh gosh, it looks like its over-baking and I should take it out right now!" Ok... never.

Well you might laugh a little at me just now, but that is OK, when I tell you I looked into my HEART today. I don't mean physically, or emotionally, or even spiritually! I am unable to explain this, but I saw what my HEART has become by just being me for these fifty-eight years.

So many events, special moments, and also supernatural blessings have overtaken me during my life; some more dynamic or overwhelming than others, but there have been many. And today when I looked into my HEART and saw the reflection of who I am was somehow uneventful. It happened like this:

I know how often I have written about my joy for working our yard and for some the repetition is boring. But there is a personal peace which exudes from within all of us when we get to do a simple but fulfilling job. There are sixteen shade trees on our property surrounded by lush green bentgrass. One unusual unknown about my mowing gear is I wear baseball cleats; metal cleats, not those soft rubber type. I, "don't fall down" when I wear them.

This afternoon I had finished the yard; edging, mowing, fertilizing, and began watering when this HEART thing happened. The shrubs, flowers, and ground cover had been clipped, racked, and watered. The one lone miniature tomato plant also received some personal attention. I guess you might call me a perfectionist if you drove by our home. ON each end of our deck area is an evergreen which seems to guard the corners.

With everything "looking good" I circled the yard for one last look before going in for a shower. As I walked around the southwest corner of our home I noticed an irregular shape of one of the evergreens. I had not paid much attention to the evergreen since they are pretty durable and do not require much attention. But the cone-shaped form of this evergreen was distorted.

As I looked at the evergreen I saw the inner most part of my HEART! The outer-shell was rigid; I needed the yard to be perfect…, but the inner core was tender and soft.

During the cold and snowy months of the winter I would awake in the middle of the night and look out my bedroom window and search the backyard for deer which visited our feeding stump. Several times I would watch a family; doe and two fawns feeding on this single evergreen. Their need to browse on tree bark and other roughage was natural. They seemed to be relaxed and I inwardly imagined safe near our home.

When I saw the irregular shape of the evergreen, I knew the deer had been returning to their safe place to feed. You must think Jim is losing it, but to know someone or something felt safe just being near was a HEART moving moment. I have often told Janice how I want to just hold someone when they seem to be hurting or lonely.

To Chew or Not to Chew: That's the Question?

Often I read the daily tabloids of business and find under the subtitles, which are designed to hide some real juicy information, a story filled with a tantalizing flavor that will cause my mouth to drop open. Today was not different!

Tucked away in the recesses of today's industry reviews was a headline which caught my eye, "The innovative and humble beginnings of roots". Chewing gum, resin of the mastic, sapodilla, and spruce trees, originated from the genius of the Greeks, Mayans and North American Indians. Later, branded chewing gum was packaged for sale to the public consumer; Tutti-Frutti was first sold in vending machines in 1888; Dentyne, sold as a teeth cleaner, was invented in 1899; and in 1914 William Wrigley Jr. added mint and fruit extracts to add flavor to a new industry of gum products.

In today's tabloid of business, Wrigley is reported to be losing not only profit margins but market shares. Why! Well, Life Savers and Altoids are not producing the expected return on investment which Wrigley hoped. I don't know about you but I consider it very difficult to chew Life Savers! Maybe Wrigley should have known that before giving Kraft 1.2 billion dollars for their "melt in your mouth" products.

I must ask again, do you chew?

I must admit I cannot remember the last time I bought chewing gum! I sometimes ask Janice, my wife, if she has some gum..., but she almost always misunderstands my request and hands me one of those triangular white pieces of horrible toasting sugar-free stuff! I think there must be a "jihad" in the "real" chewing gum industry!

I know I am not a habitual "chewer", but I really need to know; do you chew? And if so, what! I await your response..., is there a flavor called Teaberry?

Un-Forgiven Disappointments

The score was Oregon State University (2), University of North Carolina (2), and UNC had OSU down to their last out of the 8th inning. If only UNC could get the third out promptly, then UNC could rally their team hoping to score the winning run in the top of the 9th.

A powerful hit to the second baseman of UNC ended with a splendid catch and all that was left was a successful throw to the first baseman. However, the throw was wide and the runner was safe. During the recovery of the overthrown ball, an OSU runner crossed home plate and placed OSU ahead by one run.

If this was just a normal in-season game the error would be recorded in the books and the game would go forward without much fanfare. But, this was not a normal in-season game; the National NCAA Baseball Championship was at stake.

How an ordinarily simple play could become such a great DISAPPOINTMENT and would be recorded as a major failure in the minds of many, is worth discussing!

Oregon State University held on with this one-run-lead and won the National Championship, while the University of

North Carolina's team exhibited a sincere demonstration of DISAPPOINTMENT for losing the Championship.

Recently I was asked, "What is the greatest disappointment you have ever experienced?" I must admit the question caught me off-guard, since I rarely dwell upon personal disappointments for any length of time. I know my response vibrates with conceit and vanity, but really comes from a humbleness which is very difficult to explain. Let's see if I can explain my reasoning. When I experience personal disappointment, I recognize I have placed myself beyond a realistic probability of what I should achieve.

You see, it is difficult to put in plain words. For instance, if I was the second baseman for UNC I would feel an overwhelming disappointment with the throw I made. However, if my fellow teammates are true friends, I am confident each one would be disappointed in my throw, but not with ME personally. We would be included in the totality of our Alumni, those fellow graduates of UNC. One disappointing error will not destroy the totality of our Alumni!

So, in my life, I have sought to partner myself with an Alumni who are genuine in caring for all of the (one)s with the potency and support of the total. Disappointments come and go, but those which linger too long are those which have not received desired forgiveness. Most often the last one extending forgiveness is SELF!

So, "What is the greatest disappointment I have ever experienced?"… unnecessarily struggling with errors in MY life which I have not yet personally forgiven and forgotten. I need to forgive myself REMEMBERING that all of my mistakes have been forgiven by the only One who lived life without even one error.

Who knows you might want to become a fellow classmate in this Alumni… it's easy, just ask the Dean of Students.

An Ole Galvanized Bucket

Some months ago I asked Janice to purchase two items for me...; now I know you will smile or even laugh when you read about my requests. I guess as we begin to mature in age; I am not sure I have matured in action, our desires change. You know I love to work in the yard; I know I must drive my neighbor a little bite crazy since I mow our lawn at least two and sometimes three afternoons each week. During the mowing and trimming I need a wagon to move the debris to the mulch bin. Sooo... I desired a little red wagon; one like we had as a child. Sometimes Janice smiles as though she agrees with my requests, however avoiding the completion of the requested action. Don't tell Janice but I think she is saving up her money to buy the "little ole red wagon" for my birthday in November. (I guess she thinks I need to haul snow...!!!)

Janice however has already surprised me with the purchase of my second request..., an ole galvanized bucket! I still don't understand my need, wish, or even the secret desire for an ole galvanized bucket; do you have any idea why an ole galvanized bucket would even be in my memory bank? MY??? Ole galvanized bucket now rests on the southwest corner of our upper deck with one of those miniature tomato plants. I DON'T EVEN LIKE TOMATOES!

Well let's get to the reason I am writing…, I got this e-message (another one of those forwards) from our dear friend George who lives in Springfield, Massachusetts. (see below) I think he might have found why I was longing to own an "ole galvanized bucket".

During a visit to a mental hospital, a visitor asked the Director what test was used to decide whether or not a patient should be admitted. "Well", said the Director, "we fill up a bathtub, then we offer a teaspoon, a teacup and a bucket to the patient and ask him or her to empty the bathtub".

"Oh, I understand," said the visitor. "A normal person would use the bucket because it's bigger than the teaspoon or the teacup." "No", said the Director, "a normal person would pull the plug. Do you want a bed by a wall or near a window?"

Gravy

One of the pleasures Janice and I have enjoyed during our re-locations are the friendships we develop. One very special friend asked if I might put into words one particular event which could be described as "Miracles In The Kitchen".

Let me focus in on the scene. Wally, Bill T, Bill M, Richard, and I would gather together every Saturday morning to prepare breakfast for the men of Grace United Methodist Church, located in Cape Girardeau, MO. It has been said that there can be too many cooks in the kitchen, however, in this kitchen we only had one cook. Wally Sherrod was the chief cook, Bill M was the chief bottle washer, and Bill T, Richard, and I were the "hey boys".

The menu was very simple! We served bacon, sausage, scrambled eggs, fluffy hot biscuits, creamy milk gravy, fresh fruit juice, hot coffee, cold milk, pure butter, and of course many varieties of jellies or preserves. Occasionally, we would bring in a special chef who prepared pancakes.

To prepare a breakfast like the one I described, a kitchen with all of the modern equipment was a must. And we had that: two full institutional ovens, a four burner stovetop which included a large grill, unlimited pots and pans, and enough table place-settings to feed half the world. (Maybe a quarter of the world) But, there was one piece of cookware which formed the foundation to this "Miracle Breakfast".

The gravy pan was so large and heavy that only Wally could place it on the largest burner; or that is what he told us. You see, Wally was the "Gravy Maker". My job was cooking the sausage and biscuits, Bill T scrambled the eggs, Bill M made the coffee, Richard arranged the counter top for serving, while Wally made the gravy.

I can truly say Wally's gravy was the best I have ever eaten; now don't tell Janice I wrote this, she might get her feelings hurt! The details, the exact stirring motion, the timing for adding each ingredient and of course the precise temperature were all choreographed perfectly.

Each and every part of the breakfast menu had to be timed so that as the gravy was poured into all of the four previously warmed bowls, the blessing could be prayed and the serving process would begin. Gravy is not gravy if it is cold!

Our resident Bank CEO/President would speak words of wisdom almost every Saturday morning as he returned to the serving line for his second helping of scrambled eggs. "I don't get to eat eggs except on Saturday morning. Dottie says I shouldn't eat eggs; they are not good for my health!" He would smile while placing another two spoonfuls on his plate. He knew he was safe with FRIENDS!

Time spent with friends should be cherished forever!

Father's Day: 25th Anniversary

Twenty-five years ago my dad died!

Today, I look back on his life and celebrate some of the most meaningful events; some included simple verbal instructions, which continue to help me rest on a solid foundation of courage and truth.

Those of you who knew my dad might remember his physical handicap. "He limped!" For more than sixty years he believed he had suffered from the disease of polio, only later to discover polio was not his enemy. Either in birth or from an injury as a baby, his hip was somehow dislocated causing the irregular formation of his right hip and leg. "He limped."

Most people remember James Albert McClelland as one of many barbers in town, or maybe some knew him as a farmer from "turkey run", but I remember him as "daddy". My dad like starched shirts, smart looking hats, Camel cigarettes, hot coffee, and a good joke. (My dad was not one of the best story-tellers, but he enjoyed the opportunity to talk.)

Three verbal instructions are hidden deep within my inner being which came from "daddy". 1) Be sure to know that your sins will find you out...2) Never be afraid to come to me when you think you are in trouble, I will always be here to help...3) Never lie to me...we can work with the truth.

One event will always rank at #1 for me. When I received my driver's permit at the age of 14 ½ years old I received the keys to my own car. It was not NEW but it was MINE. When he handed me the keys he said these words to me, "I want you to always have enough money in your pocket and these keys to your car so you do not have to depend upon others to make decisions about where you go, when you go, or when you decide to come home"!

Some of you have shared "special" memories of your dad..., and for that I want to say "Thank You". Many of us could write pages and pages of thanksgiving for our dads' influence in our lives. I personally think all of us search every day to find ways to show our children, if we are blessed with children, how parents (fathers and mothers) can make a DIFFERENCE in their lives. So this Father's Day weekend I will be honoring my "daddy" be being the best person possible, always remembering...

1. My sins will not go unnoticed

2. Never be afraid to ask for help

3. Truth always wins

4. Never blame others for my poor decisions

Words written on paper seem to be great therapy..., you just might want to take a pencil and paper and write a "word picture" about your dad! My list had only (4) memory "truths" of MANY from my dad…, he was not perfect "He limped", but he finished life's race standing tall.

May God bless you as you Honor your dad this Sunday!

A Song Captured

The temperature will not escape the fifty's tomorrow and forty-five will mark the low temperature for Wednesday night. Fall will arrive a little early this year, the prognosticators are telling us; the leaves are changing their colors and whisper a late afternoon cool melody. Finch feeders empty daily as the migration of these beautiful birds is in full motion.

Only six steps from the coffee pot in our kitchen, is my favorite wicker rocker from which I watch the darkness of night move the evening's soft light westward. My faithful friend, the moon, is always on time each and every evening. A hen turkey and her spring hatchlings wing their way up a tall tree only 100 yards within the wooded area which parallels our back yard.

Chirping insects, croaking frogs, singing Catbirds create a harmony of sounds which cause one to smile with wonder at God's simple but complex creation. With a hot cup of coffee in one hand and the thistle bucket in the other, I walk through the moist grass toward the Finch feeders. I usually wait until the setting of the sun to fill the feeders so I will not interrupt the finches' dinner.

A gray squirrel races across the yard; I must admit it startled me just a little, making a clear path toward its hollow-tree home just inside the tree-line. He or she must have stayed at the sunflower seed feeder a little longer tonight than normal. Life seems to be enjoyable in our backyard by many varieties of wildlife and I certainly enjoy their visits.

As I refill my coffee cup and return to the comfort of my wicker rocker, the dusk to dawn lights have already awakened and send a perfect glow of light to the upper deck. As Frank, my brother-in-law, might say, "All is well in Mudville"!

Poetry, literally (creating), is a form of art many enjoy and appreciate. Speech used in rhetoric, drama, song and comedy was the original focus for writers as Aristotle. Repetition and rhyme gave was to what today's poets call "a fundamental creative act using language". What a weary definition!

Poems should expand the literal meaning of the word, or invoke emotional or sensual responses. Exciting poetry leaves an open door to the reader for multiple interpretations. When I write I tempt the reader to probe for a purpose or motivation as I "create" a question which can only be answered by the reader. Now that's exciting!

Shakespeare, Dante, Goethe, Du Fu, and Beowulf do not "wind my watch". Gilgamesh wrote on clay tablets; I prefer my keyboard. MacLeish concludes "Ars Poetica" with the line, "A poem should not mean... but be". This be too deep for me!

Many of you have read John Milton's "Paradise Lost" or Edgar Allan Poe's "The Raven". Some of you might have even enjoyed Jim McClelland's "The Face of A Child", but all of you have LIVED Bobby Vinton's "Sealed With A Kiss".

I don't wanna say goodbye for the summer
Knowing the love we'll miss
Oh let us make a pledge to meet in September
And seal it with a kiss
Guess it's gonna be a cold lonely summer
But I'll fill the emptiness
I'll send you all my love every day in a letter
Sealed with a kiss.
-Bobby Vinton

Asked which form of poetry I might enjoy best, I would not choose a Sonnet, a Jintishi, a Villanelle, a Tanka, an Ode, or even a Ghazal. I would choose what some might say is just ordinary, but I would consider extraordinary; a song captured from the heart of someone who knows the true meaning of life.

Chocolate

Everyone…, I have a wonderful and tasty test for you! Today I was reading and uncovered a most interesting impossibility. This is so unique I had to share this with you!

Simply, it is impossible to unwrap, break evenly, and allow the melting of a whole Hershey chocolate bar; piece by piece to occur within your mouth. It seems the event will create such a feeling of happiness; causing everyone to take at least one small bite or crunch between the teeth during the enjoyment of the chocolate bar.

I am a very controlled and self-disciplined person; this, I thought, would be an easy experiment. But, it's correct, sometime between the fourth and fifth small rectangular portion of the chocolate experience I did it. I could not let the melting process finalize. The most interesting find from this experience was; if you must know, was the feeling of happiness I experienced for a total failure.

Now, it's your turn to prove me wrong! I know only a few of you will go today and purchase one of those little Hershey Chocolate Bars, but the next time your eyes focus on one you will remember ME and my "failure". Try it for yourself; you will thank me for introducing you to the most enjoyable failure you have ever had.

Do something spontaneous, have some fun, laugh a little, and you can thank me later. Even though we are a little older, we can still have fun…, try it…, you will like it!

Success

Have you ever witnessed the exodus of a butterfly from its silky cocoon, or longed to skydive from a slow moving twin-engine airplane; maybe you have a better depiction of letting the inner self escape from what I call "ordinary".

I often find myself sitting on the edge of my "life" chair wanting to do more than I have ever done before, desiring to learn the art of craft of a new skill, and yearning for a higher level of worth in this life. I lean forward peering over the edge of complacency and lose my breath from the view which cascades so far below.

As I begin to describe the inner desires which often capture my daydreams, I realize that my view or perspective is out of focus. I should be leaning back in the comfort of past victories, successes, and pure satisfaction while looking upward toward an honored zeal for my future.

Deep within the recesses of our being is a life-long-dream awaiting its manifestation just as a butterfly awaits its transformation from a cocoon into a beautiful creation… to be admired, appreciated for its uniqueness, and remembered for its splendor.

I don't know the words which will be selected to describe

SUCCESS in my life during 2006; however, I have chosen to place a pen into the hand of God and allow Him to script the plan.

Will YOU join me in this journey? Together we can make a difference. My commitment to you is simple; as a word, a sentence, a paragraph, or a chapter is completed in my 2006 journal, I will share it with you. My request of you is simple; allow me to hear of YOUR successes as your journey unfolds.

Too candid...Too personal...Too scary...No, I don't think so!

Life lived to its fullness with friends is Too precious to deny!

A Kind Word Heals a Hurting Heart

Would it surprise you to know we hear thirty-two items of criticism for each item of praise! This might seem extreme; however our world is filled with extreme views and divisive differences of opinion. I wonder what might happen if we reversed this pattern for only one day! If we started offering genuine praise each and every time we observed a praiseworthy act, would we be rewarded with a day filled with less stress and/or boredom!

Our family, friends, associates, and those strangers we brush by hurriedly each day just might begin enjoying spend some time with us. Now don't be surprised, if you choose to become more complimentary than critical, when the recipients of this newly developed verbal character looks amazed or skeptical. Comments as: "What's wrong with you today, what are you up to, or excuse me, what did you say?" might be expressed.

"You sure look nice today, I really appreciate your help, or how can I help you today" are a few examples of pleasant things to say! Let's stop for just a second and develop a "nice" thing to say to _____: you choose the person. Now don't choose someone who makes time to compliment you…, choose someone who does not often share your conversations. Don't become afraid and stressed; think about that person and seek to find their unique characteristic which you sincerely admire. "ADMIRE, get real", you may be saying to yourself! Yes, everyone needs to hear a flattering word, or even more, each day!

You might feel a little strange at first once you decide to concentrate on compliments instead of complaints, but when was the last time someone looked you straight in the eye and said, "I really appreciate you"? Didn't your self-esteem improve just a little! If it is difficult to choose the first recipient of praise, let me give you a hint.

Look for someone who seems a little discouraged, overwhelmed with life, or ignored by more than a few. That's him; that's her; choose to do something nice, now! The most respectful act of appreciation you can give to another is simple, make and keep eye contact with them during a conversation. Just look for a sincere way to communicate verbal kindness to someone who needs some encouragement.

Let's keep this just between you and me! Don't tell anyone else what you have decided to do. Practice the 32 to 1 praise project and sit back; watch your life change. I know you can do it, because I know you! You are kind, caring, dependable, and most of all you have proven to be a good friend.

Someone today needs you kind words!

"I will speak ill of no man, and speak all the good I know of everybody." –Benjamin Franklin

Acceptance

Bouquets of flowers are given and received
During special occasions or while you have grieved
Bouquets are shared when words are so hard to speak
Oft times your approval, others quietly seek

Bouquets offer healing, forgiveness, and reconciliation
Words can't express our feelings in every situation
When our heart is filled with guilt or confusion
A bouquet is given, offering humble restitution

The next time flowers come your way
Look intensely at the giver and simply say
Thank you so much for you love and care
I cherish the bond both of us share

Never question the giver's intent
For the giver may give without even a hint
Of their inner need or personal desire
Just receive their gift and never ever inquire

Their purpose for giving, you may never know
The gift you return, a smile, you should always show
Never forget, bouquets utter words hard to speak
From others, your acceptance, they most often seek

Whisper's Color

Can you describe the color of a whisper
Or the language of a smile
What is the age of blue jasper
Where is the beginning of the river, Nile

Can you hear the words of a thought
Or demand the creation of a tear
What hinders the dream you once sought
Where is your passion; once so near

Can you share a secret with more than one
Or find truth apart from God
What do you fear when left all alone
Where is security, a question not so odd

Can I find peace when life is so frail
Or should I ask or even try
What should I do about betrayal
Where can I go when I need to cry

Can I dare to dream great dreams
Or is my time running out
What is my purpose, unknown to me it seems
Where is my faith when I begin to doubt

A whisper, a smile, great worth comes from within
A thought, deep emotion, eternity has no end
Secret fears given to God brings peace again
Life is worth living, for upon God I always depend

The Perfect Gift

I could give you a card to read to yourself
I could give you a photo to place on a shelf
Give you a gift which was selected with much thought
Gift a gift which without reason was bought

What must I give, I am really sincere
I'll give something that will add pleasure and cheer
You're someone special who brightens my day
Too often I'm lost without the right words to say

So I will choose a gift and wrap it so nice
I will visit the stores not just once but twice
I must be sure the gift is the one I want to send
I so hope you really like it and not have to pretend

When I've asked you directly what you might like
You just respond with a smile; with a look of delight
The sparkle in your eyes suggest I know what you want
So the gift must be just right, I need not disappoint

But now I return to the question at hand
What to give to a person who has no demand
It must be elegant but without a look of contempt
So I will give a gift only a few will attempt

I will weave together the fabric you have designed
For throughout your life you have never resigned
To give anything less than that timeless gift
Your loving encouragement is ones greatest gift

So the process has begun and it will take some time
To write the right words from that frail memory of mine
The words that best describe what you mean to me
For I don't want this gift to be a disappointment... you see

My Dad

It is a lovely afternoon here in upstate New York. The north-westerly winds are surgically removing the mature leaves from the trees which form a layer of protection over the lawn. Often I wonder about the accepted process of removing the dead leaves from the lawn; the fallen leaves might be God's design to protect the grass during the winter season. I think I will consider "mulching" all of the leaves this season rather than removing them.

We describe the beauty of each colored leaf as a wonder and gift from God as well as nature's way of viewing death. Yes, the leaves are born in the springtime and die during the fall. Sometimes it becomes more palatable to describe death with words that express change, alter, or revision of our present state. As I sit here beneath a radiant sun, enjoying a summer-like breeze, and day-dreaming, I am challenged to write about my dad. How did I traverse from falling leaves to needing to write about my dad?

Well during my most recent lawn mowing adventure I began to reflect upon my dad and how he influenced my life and the lives of others. When I am out working in our yard I seem to become unaware of my surroundings and drift off into the deepest recesses of my mind's "data bank"!

Finis McClelland, age 37 died today of "chills". This would have been the lead story of the McClelland Evening Post Dispatch if the McClelland family owned a daily newspaper in the early 1900's. "Chills", the cause of death might describe the "quivering of the body" from high fever due to an infection or pneumonia. I have always wondered about the true medical reason for my grandfather's death. My dad never had the opportunity to grow up with his dad; he was only a baby when his dad "Finis" died.

James Albert McClelland, age 69, died today of congestive heart failure. This could have been the verbal statement of friends and /or relatives as they told others of my dad's death so many years ago. I could write for hours and days about my dad, but the last day of his life will best describe James Albert McClelland.

At the age of 69, my dad still reported for work. He was a barber for almost 45 years. That morning was no different than other mornings – up early, eat breakfast (he loved his coffee), and off to the barber shop. "My customers are waiting for me", was my dad's slogan or motto! Always clean shaven, well dressed, and focused on the day's tasks, my dad never delayed to become what others might have expected him to be.

I have never been told of the names of individuals who received one or more of his services that day, but I am sure if a haircut, shave, shampoo, facial massage, or "tonic" was requested, the service was delivered professionally. The rest of my dad's last day here on earth is a remarkable "gift" to those of us who loved him so. Barbers never remove their "tool"- razors, combs, scissors, electrical clippers, etc - from the barber shop. When there was a special request to make a home-visit only the absolute necessary "tools" were taken out of the shop. But that day was different!

We are not sure the exact time my dad decided to search for a rectangular cardboard box, place each of his barber tools neatly inside the box, select a thin but strong twine string and secure the neatly folded flaps of the box. We are not sure when my dad decided to sweep the floor removing all of the hair and debris.

We are not sure what his thoughts were as he placed the "Closed" sign in the front door window and lowered the shades.

We are not sure what his thoughts were as he locked the door behind himself and walked across the street to place the "cardboard box of tools", which represented his life's vocation, on the seat of his truck. (And my dad LOCKED the truck) I wonder if he thought of his slogan or motto, "My customers are waiting for me", as he walked to Watkins Drug Store to ask one of the employees to call an ambulance. I am sure my dad knew this day would be the last day he would be known as James Albert McClelland, "the barber"!

Truly, "many of his customers were
waiting for him" in heaven.

I don't remember reading any written note, letter, or other form of written communication of my dad's...he would have never learned to type on our modern day keyboards! But the last hours of his life were filled with "Words" that can comfort any son or daughter: "I need to go now; those things which were needed to sustain life are no longer necessary. They are wrapped in a box; I love all of you and will be waiting for our eternal reunion." My dad walked from this mortal life into an eternal immortal life which all sons and daughters pray for their parents!

During the evening of visitation, many friends, family members, and acquaintances gathered to silently say goodbye to James Albert McClelland. As I stood at the door of the viewing room, Robert Flannigan suggested that this night was very unusual and he didn't know how to express just how he felt! I said, "People came to grieve and found no grief!" For truly this was a home-going celebration! My dad had been given an entire morning to prepare for his final exit from this present world. My dad took that opportunity to spend some time doing what he loved to do (give someone a haircut), discard the tools of labor he used here in his lifetime, and PREPARE to enter into eternity through Grace!

A Sleepy Blue Ocean

With an eye of caution I look on its calm
Along its shores grows trees of palm
Waves erupt spewing a salty spray
Footprints within its wake quickly wash away

Tides gently rise and predictably fall
Its cool blue color is loved by all
Treasures are hidden within its deep
Divers forever its secrets will seek

For me it's a wonder how life has survived
At depths so dark and warmth deprived
When storms are birthed and strong winds blow
I respect the warning; its power to show

As the calm returns and the waves subside
On its beaches of white sand we will abide
A warm moist breeze fills the air
All its guests have windblown hair

The ocean is calm and its color so bright
Its invitation is for the day and into the night
It screams so loud and creates such fierce motion
Never fear; it's just a sleepy blue ocean

A Candle's Flame

The brilliance of the flame pulls one toward a thought
Can it be held or experienced as a dream I once sought
Does it have a defined form or can it be measured
Can it be bought, sold, or merely treasured

Where is its origin, its beginning, or its end
Can we control it or do we even pretend
To understand its value, its beauty, or its worth

Its movement reflects within m peering eyes
I focus so intently and am captivated with surprise
It moves back and forth across life's scene
It's red, orange, blue, and every color in between

I am amazed at its strength to survive
It reduces to almost nothing and then will revive
To return to a greater and more brilliant glow

Oh to have the resilience of a candle's flame
Giving off light for others without fearing shame
Creating warmth when the day turns so cold
When in our arms someone we should hold

The brilliance of the flame pulls one toward a thought
Should I move toward that dream I once sought
Or continue in my fear of failure...I think not.

Never Fear Achieving Your Dream

Capture a Sound

Capture a sound and search for its meaning
Embrace the calm silence and find inner healing
Words spoken in anger create deep hurts
Slanderous rumor only cause false alerts

Define time as ones willingness to explore
Live life, as today is our last and no more
Dream dreams with wonder, passion, and awe
Strive for the best, don't play for a draw

Search for truth without living a lie
Compete for the win, never ever a tie
Honest and fair should be our first goal
A good reputation is better than gold

At the close of the day when others are gone
It's only you and you alone
Who must judge for yourself what is truly right
Did you give up too early or finish the fight

For me I will measure the sought-after mark
Of life's success as I fearlessly embark
On a journey that is chosen by only a few
Tomorrow blossoms into something fresh and new

So my challenge will always be the same
Did I live my life without disappointment or shame
Did I do my best with the opportunity I had
To do less than the best is oh so sad

Our Challenge

A challenge has come; climb this great wall
As I look upward I wonder; what if I should fall
I begin to climb higher; I now am mute
No one below suggested using a simple parachute

I climb higher; I've only climbed half-way
I now know the feeling of becoming the prey
I hesitate; I wonder if this is a skill
No, it's just the search for another great thrill

Now I see the peak; it's centered in my eye
Below are my peers; they're now just standers-by
I hear the encouragement from the growing crowd
I've reached the top; now I'm so proud

As I stand at the top and downward stare
My friends look up; my success they seem to share
A challenge comes from below; you must descend
I repel downward; I'm almost at the rope's end

Another challenge has come and gone
It was nice to know I was not alone
Encouragement from friends; that's always great
Now it's your turn... so don't hesitate

Max

It is this BOOK, the one I am reading whose author keeps asking me questions I don't want to answer, which is keeping me a little irritated. Some are real personal and over the years I have developed a style of my own which allows me to camouflage my weaknesses and hi-light my strengths. I know I must be the only one in the whole world who has mastered this... or am I?

Max Lucado, the author; in the future I will just call him Max, invites me to take a trip down memory lane. Everyone loves to do that, however while I am strolling he wants me to become "honest" with what I remember. That's not my style... I am not always completely forthright if it does not fit my need of the day. I know I must be the only one in the whole world who does this... or am I?

Max's first question seems OK on the surface but once captured by its true attempt to dig deep into my memory bank, I find myself a little reluctant.

"Starting in your childhood, recall times when you did something well (success) and enjoyed doing it (satisfaction)." Now that didn't hurt much, but when I did the recalling what jumped up from my memory bank was... maybe you had the same experience! What was the first thing(s) you remembered?

I know I must be the only one in the whole world who remember those things which I did not do well (failure) and those times I forced myself to do tasks which I truly did not like (dissatisfaction) just to please others... or am I?

So help me out here...

Do you recall, during your early childhood, something you enjoyed doing and that you believed you did it well?

Today's rambling is over... see you in the blackberry patch?

Windows

Windows old, Windows new, Windows
designed especially for you
Windows clear, Windows stained, Windows hidden from view
Open Windows encourage our friends to be heard
Closed Windows cause friends to pass
by without saying a word

Old Windows are stately, quaint, and so mature
New Windows are fresh, clean, and very secure
Clear Windows demand a look or even a gaze
Stained Windows whisper feelings of quiet amaze

Covered Windows should cause us to become more aware
Of ones need, ones want, or their cry for much needed care
Covered Windows often cause us to fuss or complain
Covered Windows are outward symptoms of unnoticed pain

Our life represents many Windows of time
Deep thought, contemplation, even personal opine
Which Window are you looking through today
Is it Old, Is it New, or would you rather not say

The Window I suggest you stand before
Is the Window of awe and inner adore
Of the One who gives such radiant light
Who sustains us by day and throughout the dark night

The Window is the Window of "Now"
The Window that guides us when we know not how
To move evermore quickly toward that priceless goal
As we depend upon the One who loved us so completely,
That He died to save our sinful Soul

Wildlife

I descended the eight steps which exit from our living area into the garage, reached for the camouflage clothing hanging near my work bench, and prepared for a special late afternoon visit in the wooded area at the rear of our home. From the crest of my head to the tip of my toes, using the art of camouflage, I was more or less out of sight from anyone or anything. With walking stick in hand I was off for an expedition into one of my most favorite places to visit.

Once inside the tree-line, I quietly found my way along the edge of a small corn field which is a superb feeding plot for many varieties of wildlife living alongside the small village/town of Palmyra, New York. Even though I moved slowly and quietly, a deer exited the corn field and crossed a small waterway which surrounds the wooded area. MY first sighting of my afternoon would have been enough; but let me tell you more!

Within minutes I had found my predetermined locale from which I would explore the immediate vicinity for movement of wildlife. Seated directly in front of a huge oak tree, surrounded by green leafy undergrowth, I was even more invisible to any suspicious animal or fowl. However, other residents of the woods decided to share my observation spot. Those troublesome mosquitoes swarmed just outside the net surrounding my face, neck, and ears. I think I must have smiled as they tried so hard, without success, to penetrate my flesh.

Leaves moved, limbs swayed, and the silence of the woods was broken by a fox squirrel finding his way across the dense canopy. As he jumped from limb to limb without stopping to alert others of my presence, I was comfortable that my preparation to become unknown in their neighborhood was successful. As he continued his run, another movement caught my eye.

Those of you who spend time in the outdoors hunting turkey can appreciate my next experience. The sounds of leaves moving just beyond three or four large fallen trees cause my heart to quicken its beat. Again leaves moved and the sound mimicked a sound I had heard many times before; turkeys scratching the ground searching for food. Then one of the spring turkey chicks, about the size of a chicken, slowly moved from behind the fallen trees. One by one, seven total, of these sibling turkeys showed themselves to this very thankful observer.

As I witnessed the young turkeys' dutiful search of dinner, my eyes caught another movement just over my left shoulder. A mother deer and her two fawns crossed the threshold from the corn field into the woods. I was careful not to move too quickly from one theatre, the turkeys' search for food, to another theatre, a mother deer and fawns traveling from their feeding plot to their resting area.

For almost thirty minutes I was blessed to witness wildlife in their natural state of living.

A Night in the Forest

The sun is setting now and I sit here alone
Today's warmth is leaving; my coat must go on
Young birds are called; to come to the nest
As night draws closer, it's time to rest

The darkness of day is beginning to fall
The lonely whippoorwill is sounding its call
As the horizon swallows the sun's bright light
I settle in for the long autumn night

As leafless branches open to reveal the moon
I think of a time, which will come very soon
Night's canopy will be filled by a thousand stars
If I look closely I just might see Mars

A forest's night should not give alarm
Embrace nature's beauty; if offers no harm
The moon's soft glow is ever so clear
I rest so peacefully; for I know you are near

If the darkness of life causes you concern
Just remember the forest's night and learn
Peace comes when you know in your heart
The Creator of tomorrow, His love will impart

The Plank-Board Pier

Quietly I walk across the plank-board pier
My steps are slower now; the end seems so near
A southerly breeze brings warmth to my face
I am at the pier's end now; my favorite place

An old cane-woven rocker moves in the wind
I've been here each night time and again
This place is peaceful and it allows me to think
A look up at the moon; it seems to give me a wink

As the sounds of the night begin to awaken
I recall the past; my emotions are overtaken
In my youth I dreamed of wisdom and wealth
Now that I am older I simply pray for health

Rocking alone brings very little pleasure
Visits from an old friend are always a treasure
Many nights I sit here and dream for a while
If only you would visit; that would make me smile

Time moves faster now that I'm here alone
Most days I long for the ringing of the phone
When you call, my day seems to be better
And oh how it cheers me to get a card or a letter

Quietly I walk across the plank-board pier
Back to my home; the moonlit sky is very clear
Tears begin to flow and moisten my face
You're walking toward me; I await your embrace

Walnut Trees

And I thought I had friends with lives entirely under control, tranquil and composed, trim and fit, until I got this writing assignment. Someone has more time on their hands than me..., One of YOU remembered walnut trees placed neatly along fence-rows or strategically planted parallel to country dirt roads. One of YOU recommended I might want to paint a word picture about Walnut Trees. Wow, this will take some sophisticated data mining focused toward the center of my mind's memory bank.

Well here goes!

When I think of Walnut Trees the first person I think of is "Clyde Evans". For those of you who might not have known Clyde Evans, he was not only the McClelland's postman, but everyone else's who lived in and around Monette, Arkansas. You could almost set your clock by his daily stop at the mailbox in front of your home. I don't remember the year, make, or model of his car, but I can almost hear the muffled acceleration as it drove away. I am told the most anticipated task we look forward to each day is "checking our mail". As a youngster, I recall trying to run faster than my sister to "check the mail"; it never happened, she was always faster than the little brother.

Why do I think of Clyde Evans when I think of Walnut Trees?

Just beside our mailbox was a walnut tee which dropped its fruit directly under the mailbox. Some of the walnuts would roll into the tire path which Clyde's car made and the movement of the tires over the green hull would produce a shiny shell. Clyde was the only non-family member who helped remove the green-staining hull from our walnut harvest. All the rest of us suffered with GREEN fingernails during the de-hulling procedure.

We had, I believe, four walnut trees in our yard and three along the fence-rows which bordered our family farm. As the walnuts began to fall from the trees my back began to hurt; did you ever spend a sunny early fall afternoon picking up walnuts… I did! We, I, had to pick up walnuts before I could mow the grass which was laden with leaves covered with what looked like spider webs. If I missed one, I knew it as the walnut would shoot out the side of the mower and fly through the air like a cannonball.

Removing the shell which confined the rich flavorful meat of the nut was an experience. Gosh, this is almost taking me to the very edge of my memory; I think we used an anvil and hammer to crack open the shell. Nevertheless, I distinctly remember hearing the words, "Don't hit it so hard, you will destroy the meat"! You cannot hit a walnut shell too hard; they are tough! I had to learn the technique of hitting the shell with the "just right" timing and recoil the hammer once the shell was cracked. Do you remember any of this, or am I painting the picture with wrong colors?

Now, try picturing a well buttered platter of hot chocolate fudge cooling on the counter of mom's kitchen with small mountains and valleys created by almost hidden walnuts. The temperature of the fudge had to be cooled to an exact level before cutting or too much fudge would stick to the knife. That, which would stick to the knife, I call "krinlings"! Remember the little brother who could not run very fast; I got the "krinlings".

So for YOU who suggested this "Walnut Tree" topic…, YOU can order Walnut Fudge from www.wegotfudge.com!

Spelunkers

Those of you who are spelunkers already know too well the phrase, "between a rock and a hard place". I can almost imagine the painful pressure one feels when sponged between two merging pressure points. I have never allowed myself to venture deep inside a cave or unknown cranny. But today I was forced to become engulfed by tides of others' overwhelming desire to find a place of anticipated fun. You see, during July and August a swarm of invited creatures will descend into a small corridor near Buffalo, New York.

Without thought of today's impending adventure I left my office this morning hoping to visit the Buffalo, New York marketing area to visit one of our stores. Buckled up, I looked forward to a peaceful drive.

Within a few miles of Buffalo I noticed something which gave me some alarm. The traffic normally moves about 75 mph but today the forward motion slowed to an immediate stop. How could I have been so mentally occupied to forget the annual pilgrimage of vacationers seeking an almost paralyzing pull from…"The Falls"?

Interstate 90 which dissects the heart of New York State funnels both commercial and domestic travel from New England's east coast down through the upper mid-west. Also, I-90 offers a convenient passage way from all southern states along Lake Erie into Canada. And if you could only try to imagine one southern boy right in the middle of this massive collection of road rage…, you might just smile a little!

Living in Connecticut for four years taught me an important virtue, patience! While in Connecticut we described the distance between two points in minutes and hours instead of miles. Now that we live in New York I have continued to "enjoy the trip" without trying to decipher my average MPH.

As I tiptoe down I-90 I tried to discover some amusement; I refused to become discouraged or angry. I "figuratively" placed myself inside the vehicle immediately to my right, causing to trip to become more interesting. So today, I enjoyed a robust half-smoked cigar, sat behind the steering wheel of a beautiful NASCAR automobile sponsored by Chrysler's Dodge Division, bottle-fed a new born baby while keeping a Golden Retriever from lunging over the front seat, road along with one of New York's State Troopers maneuvering between traffic to investigate a tail-gating accident, and of course enjoying a Big Mac #7 with a very hungry twelve-year-old.

As I entered the EZPASS booth, the green light signaled for me to proceed with caution. Only ¼ mile more and those "out-of-state" nice people would exit onto I-290 toward their

destination… "The Falls".

And I smiled! And I laughed! You see, within about 22 miles an exit to the Canadian border will become visible. These weary, annoyed, and hot travelers will encounter the Canadian Border Patrol Officers who have never desired a virtue called "patience".

Those nice people who have traveled so far to see... "The Falls" will become a form of traveling spelunkers; adventurers who find themselves between "a rock and a hard place".

If you long to visit Niagara Falls, call us! We will get you there contented and happy!

The Gentle Old Man

The gentle old man held softly his favorite brush
He was always patient and would never ever rush
Each masterpiece was completed with beauty and style
He painted for pleasure, always with a smile

This canvas would display his last
This one; the finale of a lift almost past
He sits for hours looking, listening, and waiting
For a visit from his child who inspired his creating

This canvas, he hoped, would become his best one ever
He would need to be focused and somewhat clever
His child was unaware of his father's future
The gentle old man was preparing for his untimely departure

Then through the dimming eyes of the gentle old man
He saw that special child reach out for his hand
It's me dad, I just thought we should talk
About the future; can we take a short walk

I've seen you create with the palette resting upon knee
Would you consider painting a simple portrait of me
It would help me remember, if you ever had to leave
How special you are to everyone... especially me!

My Friend

The path is narrow, winding, and steep
Where it leads, only a few dare to peek
There is solitude at the end of this path
A place of protection from the ocean's great wrath

A small railed fence is my only guide
Once at the top my heartbeat will subside
I rest for a while; now I must walk on
Time is precious here, and I am never alone

As I arriving in front of these swinging gates
Every muscle in my body throbs, even aches
The walk is tiresome but always refreshing
A mile or two, but I am only just guessing

The house is well kept, a beautiful landscape
A picture in my mind which will never escape
Care given to this place is without description
Only photos and memories secure its depiction

So what is the place of which I write
It's the lighthouse, which illuminates the night
The keeper of the house was a life-long friend
He was my mentor, on him I could always depend

As I sit here listening to the roar of the sea
I remember pure wisdom which he shared with me
Time helps heal my heart at the loss of my friend
My friend, My Dad, till the very end

The Rose

Your beauty and fragrance is from an ancient time
Your structure and form is complicated but oh so divine
Your inner being whispers a need for protection
Your tender petals are offered for gentle selection

In the summer of life you're oh so desired
A gentle hand for the harvest is surely required
You invite soft touches and tender embraces
Your attar births perfume loved throughout the ages

You're the rose; everyone will quietly seek
The rose desired by the strong; even the meek
You're the rose; everyone will admire
The rose I long for and forever desire

In the autumn of life when petals fade
I know, for me, you were heavenly made
For the fragrance of your love will last forever
Perpetual love blossoms as we spend our lives together

Inner Awareness

An inner awareness holds tightly to me
How precious the gift to be forever free
The thought moves so cautiously slow
Too often we resist to explore, even to grow

Time is moving faster; almost a gush
The thought is silent; almost a hush
A short hesitation will create lack or loss
Movement covers life, as moist dirt with moss

Why should we wait until the very end
The thought is real; never ever pretend
Creativity awaits the willingness of heart
When life is finished we all will depart

Will we ever imagine of holding our dream
The thought is our passion not a mere scheme
Inner desires are fleeting moments away
The best becomes less if we choose to delay

How will I find happiness or even delight
The thought becomes alive, with breath and height
Maybe a word, a phrase, or a book
Ever expanding; our dream never forsook

If I take the risk, will you come along
The thought without words, creates a silent song
Lyrics captured by music soothes a lonely heart
Your dream; your passion, you must impart

Listen for your inner calling or personal desire
The thought left inside will wither or expire
It's worth the risk; for that I am sure
Trust in yourself; you're wise and mature

An inner awareness holds tightly to me
How precious the gift to be forever free
The thought now moves evermore fast
Freedom to explore and grow is yours at last

Red Onion

From Boston, Massachusetts, where streetcars transport residents and visitors along their way, to Australia's Beef Capital, Rockhampton, those of us who take great pleasure in preparing the Perfect Cheeseburger, search for unusual condiments which will enhance our creations. The most important fact is that a Perfect Cheeseburger begins with cold fresh corn-feed BEEF.

From rare, medium-rare, medium, medium-well, and the more often served well done hunk of beef, we find a plethora of condiments which are added to create unique tastes. Some add water, evaporated milk, Worcestershire Sauce, horseradish, chives, blue cheese, sesame seeds, nuts, salt, pepper, cumin, garlic; I could go on and on!

Whatever we add to the meat, we must first select the cut of beef from which the ground is made. Maybe chuck, maybe round or even sirloin will suffice if the blending process is exact. Too much mixing causes tough burgers and allows the temperature to moderate. The blending should be done with a wooden spoon and always begin the blending in a cold metal bowl. This allows for the best chew crumble or mouth-feel.

During the cooking process, usually reaching an internal temperature of 155-175 degrees F, we must recruit another expert to facilitate with the precise warming of the buns. Buns must be warmed to a toasty golden glow, but never causing the texture of the bun to deteriorate into a too soft touch. The Perfect Cheeseburger requires an unyielding foundation which will safely guard the beef, cheese, and of course all of those toppings.

Once the beef patties are grilled to perfection, the buns are dressed with the individual's selection of mayonnaise, mustard, or that one unique sauce selected by a few gourmets. The cold cheese of your choice is added to the bottom bun…, no exceptions please.

Just within reach of everyone should be a serving tray of lettuce, tomato, pickles, and thin slices of red onions. Oh how foolish I feel now!!! One of you asked if I would write about red onions and I immediately thought of cheeseburgers.

Well maybe I can save this by just saying, "What would we be if we never experienced the flavor of the community identified as Red Onion, Arkansas?" Was is Arkansas or Missouri?

Some of the most delicious family flavors I have ever experienced like Markin, Ladd, Sipes, Berryhill, Wimpy, Wooten, Taylor, Brinkley, Farmer, and of course Floyd originated in the general proximity of a place called RED ONION.

Red Onion offered a variety of business opportunities including a restaurant, cotton gin, gas station, variety store, and the Original Barney's all-purpose mercantile. I loved to go with Daddy to the Arkansas-Missouri state line where he bought those Camel cigarettes.

I must admit I just don't know enough about the community to properly put words together to describe it. But I do know about the "PERFECT CHEESEBURGER"! I think it would be interesting if you have a tale or two to tell which would add some flavor to the Red Onion community; if so, let me know.

A Friend

In his presence you felt neither superior nor inferior; for he quietly welcomed everyone into his personal space absent of stress and discomfort. His conversation was soft as silk, but solid as forged iron. He enjoyed the exchange of receiving and giving, but his gifts were not hidden in boxes wrapped with ribbon and bows. He gave from his heart freely; expecting nothing in return.

From the first day we meet to the last day we spoke, he made me feel welcomed and cared for. His presence in a room was felt no matter the occasion. We could sit for hours without saying a word, but our conversation was filled with harmony and deep respect. He never sought power or privilege, but guided the steps of influential individuals. With calm and insightful words, he could quiet the most distasteful quarrel. He enjoyed being who God had created him to be.

He experienced loss, love, and a long life. He witnessed death, birth, and reconciliation. He was a son, father, husband, brother, uncle, grandfather, great-grandfather, and for many, "friend"!

I knew him as Dad, others knew him as Elvis, Wimp, Uncle Elvis, daddy, papa, pop, and God knew him as son! Much can be written about this man, but words only will never express adequately the attributes of a man known as Elvis Lee Poe Sr.

With honor and respect, I will always remember Dad as one of my best friends.

A Clear Night Sky

I gaze into the clear night sky
Stars hang lifeless never saying goodbye
Filling the expanse, their brilliance of color
Movement suspended awaiting heaven's divine order

Suddenly without an announcement or warning
A star seems to move, my faint hope restoring
I dream of a night with shooting stars on display
Time passes without an eruption, to my utter dismay

I gaze into the clear night sky
Requests made from within, but still no reply
If only I could witness a symphony of light
The conductor directs far from my limited sight

In a moment, in a twinkling of the eye
A beam of color races across the clear sky
I swallow deeply and my heart seems to race
As a family of stars torpedo through space

As I stand quietly under the canopy of light
I know for certain this must be the night
I witness the radiance of creation and awe
For tonight I am amazed with what I just saw

No mere dream, imagination, or powerless source
Is able to direct the stars' perfect course
No celestial body moves until the direction is given
For God is ruler on earth and in heaven

I gaze into the clear night sky
No sadness, regret, my purpose to deny
There is a plan for my life and I seek it now
For God is my Lord, and toward Him I humbly bow

Going Home

People ask me all the time, "just what do you do; I mean as a vocation"! As Janice and I enjoyed our dinner tonight at a favorite "night spot" in Newark, New York we talked a little about my week. Janice asked if I might decide to do "something else" other than what I am "doing" now. What a question! How would you answer, if given the same opportunity to respond?

This week, most of my time was focused on a Sexual Harassment investigation. The details, the sensitivity, the confidentiality, the process, and the sincere effort to find TRUTH were sometimes overwhelming. In some ways I was the prosecutor, defense attorney, jury, and finally the judge. Along with the necessity to view the information through non-bias eyes, I was unable to show compassion or disgust. To say the least, this was not fun!

Today, as I traveled to Buffalo, New York to represent our Company in a lese dispute concerning one of our store's roof failures, I witnessed a large exodus of Verizon telephone repair/ service vehicles. The untimely snow storm which paralyzed Buffalo, New York recently caused many out-of-town personnel of utility service to leave the comfort of their home and come help the clean-up process. Today, these and men and women were finally going home!

As I watched truck after truck moving eastward down I-90, I thought of two very simple but very powerful words… GOING HOME! Some of us stop "going home" earlier in life than others. Not from jobs, not from relocations, not from irreconcilable differences, but the home we knew in the past no longer exist. It's like putting shelled corn back on the cob; can't happen! So what do we do when the "home" we once knew no longer exists?

Life's Tapestry

As a tapestry becomes a great piece of art
A frame for support; is the most delicate part
New life blossoms into a person of great worth
Parents provide form at their child's birth

The loom made of hard maple makes it strong
Parents teach children right from wrong
A worthy teacher throughout your life
You taught harmony, never destructive strife

As the warps, vertical threads are added first
Your attachment to God never bent or burst
Life's image develops through endless time
Your love for me; God's idea, so divine

Tapestry's welts, horizontal threads, you add
Threads precise and strong; for that I'm glad
Life is held together using positive tension
Harmony was seen through every transition

A tapestry's image needs continual labor
Your life's image gained God's special favor
When your life's tapestry was finished
My memories of you never diminished

The Yellow Rose

In my garden are many beautiful flowers
I can relax there for hours upon hours
The sacrifice I've made to create this place
Is rewarded with beauty in every case

Bouquets taken from my garden are very nice
But within my garden one flower seems cold as ice
A little yellow rose is not showing its best
From a distance some would say it's only a guest

I wonder if the climate is too cold
Its but the blossom it would withhold
Once I thought it should be uprooted and even thrown out
But what if I hadn't taken care of it properly... I was in doubt.

I searched and searched for an answer
to my troublesome concern
I would do whatever necessary to fix it if only I would learn
What mistake I had made, I'll change and give it a chance
Just to fulfill its natural desire to blossom;
my garden to enhance.

As I longed for how I could help this little yellow rose
Information came to me and the answer was disclosed
It needs plenty of space to develop if I expected it to grow
It's a "greedy feeder", I must feed it if its blossom is to glow.

So I prepared a spacious spot filled with nutritious soil
I tilled the soil over and over never minding the toil
For this little yellow rose was a special gift for me
I desired to see it flourish and its buds open for all to see.

My Sister

She's part of my family and oft times I forget
To tell her I love her; for that I regret
My day moves so fast; there's so much to do
I should call her; just say I love you

She's part of my family and oft times I forget
To send her a note; for that I regret
My day moves so fast; she knows I care
I'll write her a note, current news to share

She's part of my family and oft times I forget
To spend time together; for that I regret
My day moves so fast; I do miss her so
I'll make time today; time's wasting I know

She's part of my family and she's special to me
She's my sister; and it's so very plain to see
We're part of a family, and forever we will be
Special to each other for the whole world to see

Made in the USA
Columbia, SC
21 October 2017